STOP SMOKING

The Keys To Finally Stopping The Habit Of Smoking That You've Always Wanted Cigarette Smoke Is Bad For You Nowadays, Natural Ways To Quit Smoking

(You Can Finally Kick The Habit Right This Second With Our Revolutionary New System)

Gabriele Neumeister

TABLE OF CONTENT

Introduction 1

Methodology Three brief statements ... 33

Gains From Giving Up Smoking 41

Methods And Structures For Quitting Smoking 53

Establish A Clear Goal About Smoking 66

What Makes You Want To Give Up Smoking? 85

The Advantages Of Maintaining Your Quit Smoking Habit 95

Introduction

Tobacco product cravings and a range of physical and psychological symptoms can accompany the challenging process of quitting smoking. Deep breathing is a vital technique that can help you transition into a more positive emotional frame of mind when you are feeling agitated or anxious due to nicotine withdrawal.

Inhaling fresh oxygen into the lungs is a great approach to enhance both your physical and emotional well-beingwellbeing. This is especially helpful while your lungs are healing from the adverse effects of smoking. Practices involving deep breathing are a great way to remind yourself that you can still be calm and relaxed after quitting smoking.

As smokers are well aware, cravings for cigarettes can occur at any time and without warning. On the other side, being ready for certain circumstances can help you avoid giving in to temptation when it does present itself. One primary method that works well at any time and doesn't require any extra equipment is deep breathing. If you pay attention to the rhythm of your breath, you can refocus your attention from that bothersome craving into a place of tranquility.

Think about making use of this book to practice some basic breathing exercises. It can help to imagine the ideal breathing rate—not too fast, not too slow, measured and under control—in order to keep control over your breathing.

According to the results of the study described above, deep breathing exercises have been demonstrated to lessen "smoking withdrawal symptoms, such as a craving for cigarettes," as well as the tension and anger that accompany them.

By consuming more oxygen, deep breathing can also make you feel more alert and enhance your capacity for concentration.

Try out several various approaches to find the one that works best for you.

The book goes into great detail on how a few easy techniques can be a great addition to your toolkit for managing anxiety, preventing a relapse, and generating the breathing space you need when life gets too much to handle.

By taking a few minutes to regulate your breathing deliberately, you can much help to calm the terrifying storm of a full-blown panic attack if you're being pulled into it by an unbearable grip of growing anxiety. If you set aside some time to practice mindful breathing control, you can really help to calm that storm. Just taking a few minutes to practice conscious breathing control can go a long way toward soothing a shower.

It is possible to breathe slowly, deliberately, and regulated to bring about a sensation of calmness inside yourself. By doing this, you'll be able to manage the circumstance instead of letting your anxiety rule you.

On the other hand, you can breathe via your nose.

Many people find that their thoughts and feelings are so overwhelming that they are almost immobile; in these cases, it could be helpful to focus on the specific action needed to perform alternate nostril breathing.

This is an explanation of how it functions:

The first and most important thing to do to prepare yourself for this exercise is to take a long, deep breath.

2: Permit your mouth to loosen, your shoulders to drop back again, and your muscles to loosen up a little bit.

Using the tip of your right thumb, press on the inside of your right nostril.

You can relax by inhaling profoundly and calmly through your left nostril.

As an alternative, you can toggle by pressing your left index finger against the inside of your left nose.

Step number six is to inhale deeply via your left nostril.

American Facts About Tobacco
More males than women smoke.

Compared to other ethnic groups, smokers are more prevalent among American Indians and Alaska Natives.

Those from Asia and the Pacific Islands and Hispanics are more likely than others.

Americans of Korean descent Compared to straight men, gay and lesbian men smoke more frequently.

Smoking rates are lowest among people who are 16 years of age or older, educated, and belong to middle-class and upper-class demographics.

It should be understood that this is about the degree of harmfulness rather than complete eradication. Giving yourself a break really helps to reduce some of these symptoms, allowing you to shift your attention from the physical side of quitting to the psychological side of things. Numerous options start to surface gradually. Nowadays, nicotine-free lozenges (Chantix) and nicotine-containing nasal sprays and inhalers (Zyban) are also accessible. How do you operate? They attempt to slow down the body's synthesis of nicotine. It is designed to release nicotine into the body at a precise rate, just like the nicotine patch. The primary distinction is that nicotine from patches lasts a few hours, whereas nicotine from cigarettes reaches the bloodstream and lungs instantaneously. Instead of a rapid withdrawal, the body reacts to a delayed effect as intake actually drops. Homeopathic medicineCompounds in homeopathic smoking cessation treatments become pretty helpful once you stop smoking. We strongly advise you to speak with a physician before selecting any such product because the ratio may be harmful.

Answers to Common Questions: Is it essential to give up smoking? It's not just necessary but imperative to give up smoking if you love yourself and your coworkers. Is a Longer Life Guaranteed by Quitting Smoking? It's possible that only God can ensure human life. But in a world where calamities and flaws have crept into every aspect of life, giving up smoking can undoubtedly help you minimize issues. Can my family be affected by smoking? Of course, yes. Your family members, including your children, start smoking passively and run the danger of contracting hundreds of ailments.

Furthermore, one must never overlook the financial element. You run the risk of teaching your kids to follow you as well, so keep that in mind. Can I manage tension or stress without smoking? Relieves tension in cases of mental distress. Nicotine only makes your urges go away. A far better option if you truly want to release your anxiety, stress, or strain is meditation. After I stop smoking, can I still focus? When you genuinely wish to smoke, the aftereffects only last a brief while. Long-term habit is the primary psychological cause of it. However, it's only going to take a few days. As an alternative, you might use toothpicks or candies.

Your 10-Step Plan To Quit Smoking

You have decided that it is time to stop, and you cannot change back. You've looked into every detail there is to know about the hazards to your health—or maybe just a few pieces from your doctor will do—and you know that this is the best course of action.

Right now, what exactly?

As they say, choosing to give up is actually half the battle. Many smokers talk about quitting, and many actually do intend to do so, but many never follow through on their plans. Congratulations on doing this much on your own.

Step 1: Create a factors checklist.

Do that right now if you haven't already, as we have really instructed. Take out a pen and paper, list those aspects, and make your outline as detailed as possible. If you're concerned that secondhand smoke may affect your children, write it down and include their names to make it more personal.

It takes more than just deciding to reach the surface line. And this is where we could help right now. The ten steps listed below are necessary to ensure that your plan to quit will be successful.

Make a list of the health and wellness risks associated with cigarette smoking if you're concerned about your wellbeing. Draw up all the cancer cells associated with smoking cigarettes, not just the ones related to lung cancer. Here are a few pointers now:

Step 6: Ask for your help in the appropriate position.

Don't let the opportunity pass you by; instead, decide on a concrete plan of action for today.

Take a look at your schedule right now and decide which day you want to start living your life according to the principles you have actually chosen. And what about in three days?

Step #4: Create a list of substitutes.

You also need to include the people in your immediate vicinity who are affected by your cigarette smoking in your list of variables. Are your children consuming smoke from you? This affects your animals as well; therefore, talk about their wellbeing and health as well!

Step #2: Create a piggy bank account or open a savings account.

What about those hobbies you're going to enjoy, like woodworking or knitting? Are all of your items in alignment? Do you have a space in the den reserved for it, if it's a version or a tiny structure?

The thing is that you should have that vision in your head, especially when you are first starting, to motivate yourself to move forward. Once the money has really increased, you can then clearly decide what you intend to finish with that account or that piggy financial institution.

As each year goes by without a cigarette, you should celebrate your stop day just like you would any other wedding anniversary. To commemorate this important day, send yourself a card, go out to dinner with your family, disappear for the weekend, or do something very different. In any case, could you not put it off any longer?

It certainly isn't enough to want things to end. To ensure that you carry out your goal, you need a well-defined plan, and choosing a day is essential.

Some people wait for important occasions, like their birthday or New Year's Day, or whatever. However, make sure to put off your decision for a while.

Additionally, if you and your partner—or you and a friend—are breaking up, then ask them to take care of this. While you and your friend were only contrasting notes, you and your partner could create a joint account. Additionally, you might use this money to fund your incentive system when you reach specific milestones or turning points. For example, you could use it to go shopping together, indulge in a special meal, or engage in any other activity that is special to you both.

Tell everyone you know about your plans, including your spouse, friends, coworkers, other family members, kids, and anybody else you think of. Have an honest conversation with folks who are close to you about your goals and how you need their assistance.

Do you find it concerning that the tobacco industry has been around for a long time despite the adverse and perhaps deadly effects of smoking cigarettes? Do you find it troubling that your money is going to these shady characters instead of your child's college fund, your IRA, or that new set of jet skis or vacation log house you've always wanted?

Cancerous cells in the larynx, esophagus, and mouth. The risk of dying from laryngeal cancer cells is 20–30 times higher in heavy smokers than in non-smokers. Cigarette smoking has been linked to around 57% of cancers in men that affect the mouth and vocal cords, 54% of oesophageal cancers, and 73% of laryngeal cancers.

Bladder cancerous cells. The smoking of cigarettes has been linked to bladder cancer cells in 36% of women and 43% of men.

Cancerous kidney cells. Smoking is, at the very least, a contributing factor and may even be the primary cause of the formation of kidney cancer cells in the parenchyma.

Pancreatic cancerous cells. It is stated that smoking cigarettes is responsible for 24% of pancreatic cancer cells in males and 19% in women.#4.

Belly cancerous cells. It is estimated that smoking cigarettes may be linked to 14% of stomach cancer cells in men and 11% in women.#4.

Cancerous cells in the vulva and cervix of the uterus. Women who smoke are more likely to develop cancerous cells in their cervix and vulva.

Penis cancerous cells. It's been reported that smoking causes 30% of penis cancer cells.

The rectal cancer cells. Overall, smoking cigarettes is the cause of 48% of rectal cancer cells in males and 41% in women.

Blood cancer cells, including multiple myeloma and leukemia. Research has been gradually linking smoking cigarettes to specific types of leukemia since the mid-1980s.

Liver cancerous cells. A growing body of research suggests that smoking cigarettes may pose a hazard to liver cancer cells on its own.

cells from prostate cancer. Although the formation of prostate cancer cells has not been linked to cigarette smoking, smokers may be more vulnerable to more aggressive conditions or cancer cells that progress more quickly. According to a recent study, current smokers have higher prostate cancer cell-related death rates.

If not, now is the moment. Will you take a walk around the neighborhood? Are you putting away the meals that need to be cleaned at this particular time?

Third Action: Choose a day.

How Much Do You Want ?

But, can you truly stop? Allow small time's story to give the last proof that you can.

Wilhelm is an extreme ex-trader marine commander who quit following 30 years of smoking. He comes out with the simple truth of the matter.

"You just need to stop. It would help if you concluded that you're done. You should get to the heart of the matter where you disdain every little thing about it. Up to that point, you'll concoct reasons to smoke... My canine kicked the bucket, I had an intense day at work, my ex exploded the house, whatever... When I understood I was a captive to smoking, I realized I needed to stop. I loathed the consistent smell on my garments, the desire for my mouth, the stained fingers and teeth... .I returned home on a Friday late evening [having settled on the choice to quit].... Following 24 hours, it was unpleasant. It hits you like a block. I had been resting to attempt to forget about it. I woke up and ate a whole chocolate cake—irately! Then, at that point, I dropped in a chocolate daze. At the point when I woke up Sunday morning, I looked at the mirror and said, 'I'm a non-smoker.'"

At the point when you're attempting to stop, the traditional guidance is to shape new propensities to supplant the old ones you recently connected with smoking—drinking a brew with a companion, for instance, or staring at the TV. "I attempted that," says Wilhelm, "for about seven days in the wake of stopping. And afterward, I thought: This is wild. No other movement or propensity can make me get another cigarette. At the point when you quit smoking, that is the fact: you're not generally subjugated to the cigarettes."

That was just about 10 years prior. Wilhelm still needs to get one more cigarette from that point forward.

How come we keep going back, knowing what we know about Mr. T.? How does he control us? Most smokers have, at some point in the past—or perhaps hundreds of times—made the firm determination to give up smoking and never look back. They've had enough of Mr. T. They're so tired of him since he's been treating them so poorly for so long. They come to the permanent conclusion that they are done with Mr. T.

It is also a real decision at the moment. An actual choice.
And this was the proper choice. It seems like "This is the real me making this decision" at that moment never to pick up Mr. T. again. In all time!
After an hour, day, or week, it seems as though the "me" that was before has changed. A "me" who, despite Mr. T.'s cruel, erratic, and brutally abusive behavior, genuinely misses him. Driving around the neighborhood, we find ourselves getting closer and closer.

What the Hell, oh. He's there. We make a stop. We sneer and say, "Come on." Come on in.

So where was the real me, the driver, who had only moments before said, "That's enough," at that very moment? I'm through. I've had enough of him. I'm never going to pick him up again! We feel like totally different people—at least for the moment—when we give in to smoking than when we were me, "the decider," who had made the apparent decision to give up not too long before. How does this personality transition take Place? How come in so little a time, we feel so totally different?

    The majority of us attribute this "switch" from no to yes to individual weakness, a lack of willpower, or being so dependent on these things that we are unable to maintain our straightforward resolve to stop. After considering it for a long time and working with numerous strong, extremely competent, and accomplished people who are in a similar situation, I would argue that our decision to go from no to yes is actually the result of a subtle shift in our inner identities rather than a lack of willpower, weakness, or wild addiction.

Whether or not they smoke, it's a widespread, everyday, and noticeable transformation that everyone goes through. The secret to breaking free from Mr. T will become apparent to us after we figure out how this switch is switched on and off.

How, then, can one turn on and off the "identity switch"?

Once more, it all boils down to one word: awareness.

How Focus Is Operated

It's clear that Mr. T. has our full attention and won't let go. Thus, let's ignore Mr. T. and smoke for the time being and focus solely on attentiveness.

(Yes, if you would like, you are welcome to smoke as we pay attention.)

This is how focus functions: Everything that captures our interest tells a tale. The narrative evokes an emotion. The

emotion prompts a response. And in less than a second, all of this is possible.
It appears as follows:

Interest, Subject, Narrative, Emotion, and Action

Focus on anything in the room where you are reading to help visualize and maintain the realness and simplicity of this. If you focus on something like a photo, a memento, or a recent purchase, the process will become more evident. It can be something as simple as a plant, lamp, or coffee cup. Suppose you focus on a picture of your father.
All of the stories we have about our father instantly surface when we focus on such a picture or such an item. In the event that we have a close, loving relationship with him, these stories will also make us feel cozy and reassured. Should our bond not have been so comfortable and consoling, the tales and emotions would be more ambiguous and problematic. In any case, we can then choose to take action, which could

include phoning, not calling, emailing, or, in the event that he has died away, calling or emailing a sibling. If the relationship was very stressful, we might take the decision that the damned photo shouldn't be kept out all the time.

The straightforward idea here is that memories, emotions, and behaviors—including avoidance or inaction—are evoked when we gaze at the picture of our father.

A thousand times a day, this exact procedure takes Place. We focus on something, and that "something" evokes memories, emotions, and behaviors. It could be anything as simple as a sink full of dishes, valuable something like our most recent bank statement, or something significant like a letter from a former romantic partner. Our attentional focus is the foundation for all stories, emotions, and behaviors.

Alright, let's take a closer look. Our emotions and ideas shape our narratives. We begin to identify with the same stories—thoughts and emotions—when they recur repeatedly and repeatedly. In actuality, most of us place more often with our fleeting thoughts and feelings than with the more fundamental self from which all of our thoughts and feelings originate. Our inclination to identify more with passing ideas and sensations than with existence itself is a quaint, outdated perspective on both our inner and outside experiences. All sorrow stems from this restricted affiliation with our fleeting thoughts and sensations. However, I'll talk about this in my next book, How to Stop Suffering in Fifteen Easy Years.)

Our stories become the foundation of our identities. "I'm a mommy or a dad," "I'm a Green Bay Packer fan," or "I'm not a morning person." And then this identity appears anytime our gaze lands on something within that realm.

It appears as follows:

Identification

Focus, Subject, Narrative, Emotion, and Action

Feelings

Based on our stories, each of us possesses a plethora of these identities that surface depending on the situation, such as when someone calls our attention to them. We have several identities, including those related to politics, spirituality, our "body," finances, sexual orientation, families, tax preparation, and much more. Most of the time, our many identities are silent, undetectable, and inactive until they are "awaken" when we focus on something.

It's interesting how these identities can vanish just as fast as they emerge. When a lovely girl passes by and flirts with her hips, a group of guys may be sitting about discussing last week's football game, sharing and enjoying one other's roles as "football analysts." The "lady appreciation identity" quickly takes the Place of the football analyst persona (for the majority of the guys). The "here I am working hard" or "here I am getting back to work" identities instantly replace the football analyst identity and the girl appreciation identity if the boss steps into the room when the guys were meant to be working.

My Opinion Regarding Chantix

Alright, please provide a brief disclaimer before sharing my thoughts.

Giving up smoking is the aim. I tell you straight up, "For God's sake, get some help!" a few pages back. That's okay if taking a prescription drug gets you there. I don't think it's required, but if you really need it, then it's necessary.

That serves as a warning. The details are about to get real, with a large but and a dose of however.

Why bother if all you end up doing is substituting one addiction for another? It's the main idea. Think about methadone for a minute. What makes that a brilliant idea? You're clean from heroin but addicted to methadone; when you attempt to stop taking the methadone, you find yourself using heroin again. terrible cycle.

Thus, Chantix, a medication of a class of drugs for quitting smoking, is available for purchase.

According to Wikipedia, it's a smoking cessation aid. In other words, it assists but does not perform the task. With that part, I'm fine. This is where I get into trouble:

Key Safety Information:

When taking Chantix to help them stop smoking, some people have had hostile, agitated, sad, or suicidal thoughts or actions. Some patients experienced these side effects from the moment they started using Chantix, while others didn't have them until several weeks into the medication or after quitting. Chantix should be stopped immediately and you should call your doctor if you experience any of the following: mania, abnormal sensations, hallucinations, paranoia, confusion, aggressive feelings, depression, agitation, or hostility. Prior to using Chantix, disclose to your doctor any history of depression or other mental health issues, as Chantix may exacerbate these symptoms."

Right now, are you effing kidding me? Is this a joke or an SNL sketch of any kind? As someone who has seen it firsthand, how would you characterize a shift in behavior characterized by hatred, impatience, and melancholy? You can relate to that if you have ever gone nine hours without smoking. REMOVABLE!!!

I might also want to commit suicide when taking this. I'm trying to stop smoking here, folks, from where I am! I want to live, so I want to stop! Having given up smoking and preventing the progression of lung, prostate, throat, mouth, heart, and emphysema cancers, I am now trying to prolong my life since I have at last discovered a bit more love for myself. (laughing deeply) Why, then am I holding a gun to my head?

Let's be clear about one thing right now. I was hostile, irritated, depressed, worried, panicked, excessively aggressive, angry, and manic during withdrawals. In addition to being extremely confused, I experienced angry and suicidal thoughts, strange feelings (like breathing more accessible), and slight hallucinations. So, could someone please tell me what this medication is worth? From my vantage point, even if you quit entirely, will you still have to put up with all of this garbage?

Thus, to make matters worse, using this medicine may also cause a potentially fatal rash. I could have an allergic response and swell my face. My breath supply might also be cut off if my lips and throat enlarge in the same way. I'm meant to stop taking medication and notify my doctor as soon as I experience any of these symptoms or if I develop a rash that peels or blisters in my mouth.

Truly? That's wise counsel, then!

For myself, I'll take periodontal problems and ashtray breath over this nonsense. But hold on, things improve! The most frequent adverse effects, it seems, are vomiting, nausea, constipation, gas, and sleep issues.

FIRST CO-WORKER: "Hey Bob! How's your day going?"

BOB: "Well, Cheryl, this animosity just keeps building up inside of me, and I'm quite irritated for no apparent reason.

I'm having anxiety and am becoming more and more depressed. So much so that when I finish those reports for Sam I Am, who keeps telling me it's okay and peering over my shoulder, I'm considering jumping off the roof. I am not talking about Jack or Bobby when I say that my spleen is vibrating, which I believe is somehow directly tied to the Kennedy assassination. Ed was thrashed, you have to admit that! However, Julie, I'm pleased you inquired about my health since I believe I have a rash on my tongue, but I can't seem to see it because I'm so queasy that I'm frightened to open my lips for fear of throwing up once more. I'm beginning to swell, and I'm not sure if this is just gas or a reaction. You are aware that the Russians are adding something to the water that restricts your ability to urinate to once every third Saturday of the month? I discovered that through a dream I had, and you know who deduced that information and put his trust in me— Woody Woodpecker. But wait! I haven't smoked in six days! I'm going to go down the stairs and give that forklift a try."

Visualization is a very well-known and highly successful technique that lets you visualize what you desire and, in doing so, helps you to believe as though it is indeed attainable and then actually make it happen.
We can only believe something is practical and attainable because we have seen it in our minds. It all comes down to comprehending how it operates and really mastering this strategy. With some evidence, we can succeed with ease; in fact, most individuals find mental imagery to be easy, while some people may first experience some problems.
If visualization is a challenge for you, try selecting a basic object, observing it, and then closing your eyes to try viewing it, or close your eyes and allow your mind to image a thing of your choosing, allowing it to explore freely and silently. You will undoubtedly succeed quickly.

One of the best human abilities is the capacity to visualize and imagine things. Everything that was created had to have first been envisioned, then visualized, and finally realized.

Therefore, all you need to do is follow these easy steps: 1. Give yourself all of your motivation! To persuade yourself, express your desire. For instance, you could say out loud or in your head, "I want to start breathing now!" or "From now on, I will breathe only clean air!" or "I want that my lungs be clean again!" without making any mention of smoking or cigarettes. Select the phrase that best expresses your desire to stop smoking, and make sure it is clear, concise, and direct. Should

When the wish is communicated authentically, good vibes will come over you.

2. Assemble one or more images that are connected to your desire; the image must originate from you because it is intimate. You can envision yourself, for instance, exhaling deeply of clean air or

discarding a pack of cigarettes. Use any image that will enable you to achieve your goal.

3. Make the picture better. Please place it in the fire and play around with the size, clarity, brightness, and color until it strikes your fancy and feels exactly right.

4. Let go of the picture. Now unwind and resume your regular activities. It would help if you felt confident and at ease that your goal and the vision you have generated will serve you well and permanently divert your attention from smoking cigarettes.

For several days, repeat these actions. Do it in the morning and evening. It will take a minute or two in the latter case, but you can take longer if you have more time. You'll discover that visualization is a potent tool that can help you visualize where you want to be in the future and how to get there. By employing this method, your internal feeling of positive energy will increase and your desire to smoke will completely vanish; day by day, the effects will become more noticeable.

We can combine the imagery with another potent method: brief sentences.

Methodology Three brief statements

It is vital to choose our words carefully because others will hear them, and they may have a positive or negative impact.
Gautama

This method is relatively easy to use, quick to apply, and capable of producing excellent results. This method should be applied ideally prior to smoking in order to prevent lighting the cigarette.

All you need to do is select a succinct and impactful sentence to repeat, walk away, and stop thinking about smoking.

I'll give you an example to help you understand how this works: if you get up in the morning and your first instinct is to light a cigarette, you need to be ready with a positive statement that you can repeat to yourself to help you break this habit.

Break this natural behavior right away to regain your freedom.

It must be a pleasant, likable, and happy-making sentence. Examples of such corrections include "The first thing I like to do when I wake up is to open the window and breathe deeply" and "...is drinking freshly squeezed orange juice." These are only examples; the term you choose must assist you in immediately breaking the negative module and providing a genuine energy boost rather than a phony one, like cigarettes; you have a lot of options.

It would be best if you repeated this to yourself silently or out loud in a clear, assured, secure, peaceful, and relaxed manner, using a pleasant, even seductive, and convincing tone of voice. Once you have expended all of your energy, you can utter the phrase once or more times.

Determine other instances during the day when you feel the need to smoke automatically and have some phrases ready to help you break the pattern of your smoking habit.

This approach is particularly successful since it can be applied quickly and shortly before smoking, which is the ideal time to use it. It takes some time to work, so if you smoke and don't know why, don't worry about it. It's just a part of the process. If you keep using the short sentence strategy with minor adjustments—you can use a different phrase or repeat the word multiple times—you will be able to break the habit and regain your freedom quickly.

You can also employ a mantra, which is a statement you can repeat to yourself whenever you want, to help you in any scenario. Use your favorite sentence, "I love to breathe only clean airYou can now proceed to study the following method! We must set up an incentive or reward because we can't always be too harsh with ourselves.

DAY-TO-DAY IMPLICATIONS OF SMOKING

Your body is increasingly vulnerable the more you smoke. Moving closer to a smoker increases the risk of inhaled smoke for nonsmokers, as there is a higher risk of lung cancer for nonsmokers who regularly inhale smoke.

2. Heart Conditions In America, heart disease is on the rise, and 20% of those who suffer from it have smoked in the past. Due to the fact that the heart is a mechanical organ that circulates blood throughout the body, smokers are more susceptible to heart disease. As a result, blood that has been altered or

contaminated travels directly to the heart and is then distributed throughout the body.

3. Diabetes: Type 2 diabetes has been linked to smoking. Compared to the average nonsmoker, smokers have a higher risk of developing diabetes. Those who smoke and have the illness, however, make it far more challenging to treat and manage.

4. Ineffective Penis Smoking causes plaque to accumulate in the arteries, obstructing blood flow.

The blood cannot get to the locations it is meant to since the regular blood flow is abruptly stopped. Both men and women experience this problem, which makes sexual interactions more challenging.

5. Ectopic Pregnancy: When a woman conceives, but the pregnancy does not develop inside the womb, it is called ectopic pregnancy.

When an egg is fertilized in a Fallopian tube, this is typically the most likely outcome. Pregnancies of this kind that entail smoking are becoming more and more prevalent.

6. Liver Cancer: As you may already be aware, smoking is bad for your health. In this instance, smoking has a significant adverse effect on the PH level of the liver, increasing the risk of liver disease in smokers.

7. Loss of Vision Smoking raises the risk of glaucoma, cataracts, dry eye syndrome, and diabetic retinopathy, according to several studies conducted over the years.

8. Tuberculosis Research has indicated that individuals who have previously had treatment for tuberculosis are twice as likely to contract the disease again.

9. Bladder cancer: This is a condition that is beginning to grow more and more quickly. An increasing number of people

are starting to get bladder cancer. You guessed it: smoking is one of the factors contributing to the rise in bladder cancer cases!

10. Stroke: Picture yourself attempting to sip a thick milkshake using a straw. Think about how hard it would be to down that milkshake. That's the physical effect of smoking. The blood becomes more comprehensive from smoking, akin to a milkshake, and the blood vessels resemble straws. The damage eventually makes its way to the brain, where it causes a stroke.

11. Secondhand smoke: According to the Environmental Protection Agency, secondhand smoke is an agent that can cause cancer. This implies that exposure to cigarette fumes alone can result in some severe health problems, even in those who do not smoke cigarettes. In the US, secondhand smoking aggravates asthma, resulting in an estimated 3400

deaths from lung cancer annually, 42,000 deaths from heart disease, and approximately 150,000 to 300,000 lower respiratory tract infections.

Gains From Giving Up Smoking

The moment is now to give up smoking. However, in order to maintain your decision, you do need to give it some thought. You will discover, however, that you are indeed doing yourself a favor as soon as you decide to stop.

Nicotine has a limited amount of time to remain in the body. You will go through withdrawal symptoms when you stop since nicotine leaves your body gradually. We've covered this in detail in the earlier s, but in order to fully appreciate the advantages of quitting smoking, you need to know that this mechanism is crucial.

Within twenty minutes of quitting, your blood pressure starts to go back to normal, your pulse rate goes back to normal, and the temperature of your feet and hands increases and goes back to normal >) Within eight hours of quitting, the level of carbon monoxide in the blood drops to normal levels and the amount of dissolved oxygen in the blood stream rises to normal >) Within twenty-four hours of quitting, the risk of having a stroke or a heart attack starts to decrease >) Within forty-eight hours of leaving, you will experience a heightened sense of smell and taste, the nerve endings in different parts of the body begin to grow and regenerate, and the by-products of nicotine in the body are entirely removed from the system >) Within seventy-eight hours of quitting, breathing becomes more accessible and the bronchial tubes are beginning to relax >) Within two to twelve weeks of quitting, you will find out that aerobic exercises and walking becomes a lot easier >) After a month, the circulation of blood significantly improves and you will have more energy >) After one to three months, the function of the lungs will increase by up to thirty percent, the cilia in the bronchial tubes begin to regenerate, the lungs start to become cleaner, and the chance of being infected is reduced >) Sinus congestion, coughing, shortness of breath, and exhaustion significantly improve after one month to a year. The total risk of getting COPD can be lowered by at least five percent after two to four months. After two years, your ability to recover significantly improves, your chance of dying from heart disease is lowered by twenty-four percent, and your recurrent ulcers will eventually heal. After a year, the risk of developing coronary heart disease would have decreased by at least fifty percent. Three years later, the risk of a heart attack or stroke is comparable to that of someone who has never tried smoking at all. Ten years later, pre-cancerous cells are totally removed and are replaced by normal, healthy cells. Fifteen years later, the risk of lung cancer is equivalent to that of a person who does not smoke.

The societal advantages of quitting smoking include>) Lower health insurance premiums if you pay for any coverage >) Greater control over your life's circumstances. Your family won't be sick from the secondhand smoke you regularly expose them to, which will boost your self-esteem significantly. Moreover, your appearance will be healthier, making you appear more appealing.

The particular advantages that women enjoy are as follows: >) The chance of fetaldeath is significantly decreased for those who abstain from smoking for the whole nine months of pregnancy; >) The likelihood of giving birth to an underweight child is minimal for those who stop smoking three to four months before becoming pregnant; >) The risk of cervical cancer is decreased two years after quitting. Menopause often occurs two years later in non-smokers.

The particular advantages that elderly folks experience are as follows: >) Smokers have more excellent rates of physical disability >) Nonsmokers have better self-perceived health status >) Seniors who smoke typically have higher rates of depression.

The striking shift in average lifespan: Take note that an individual's life expectancy is roughly the same as that of nonsmokers if they choose to stop smoking before the age of 35. Individuals who decide to give up smoking between the ages of 35 and 65 often see an increase in life expectancy of five years. Those who choose to give up smoking later in life could anticipate living an extra year over those who choose to stick with it.

THE THREE SMOKER TYPES

The explanation is that this particular smoker is aware of his history of abuse and understands that he will eventually have to quit smoking in order to avoid potentially dire repercussions. He is compelled to leave since he values nothing more than smoking, and because he became deeply dependent on cigarettes, his conscience has been troubling him the entire time.

The second category of smokers consists of those who purchase a pack every day and finish it all, never going over or under. Because he is exceedingly astute and aware of his limitations, he is regarded as the second most challenging to stop. This is explained by his self-control when it comes to smoking; by using this method, he feels confident that he can continue to smoke cigarettes for the rest of his life. He consumes the right foods to counteract the consequences of smoking. To put it mildly, he is brilliant.

The third category of smokers consists of occasional smokers, who are often observed in social settings such as clubs on the weekends. He prefers to smoke in social situations. Therefore, he only lets himself smoke when he's around other people. He merely wants to smoke in order to be seen; he doesn't want to be associated with smoking. He does not smoke habitually and approaches tobacco in a very unique way. He is quite astute in his approach and doesn't smoke when he wakes up or has his morning coffee.

In summary, due to his habits and conviction that he doesn't smoke, he is considered to be the least likely to quit.

SETTLEMENTS WITH RELATIVE WEIGHT GAIN

A common concern among those considering quitting is the possibility of gaining weight. This is especially true for women since giving up smoking can lead to weight gain. The reason for this is that eating is typically substituted for smoking. The good news is that even though you may temporarily gain weight, your newly established "post-smoking plan" will help you lose the extra weight you gained when you stopped smoking.

You will eventually notice that you are becoming more physically active, enjoying outside activities and going for brisk walks or jogs. It will enable you to avoid gaining weight. You will be able to see a more exciting and enjoyable version of yourself if you take up hobbies in place of merely sitting and smoking or standing and smoking. The extra weight gained after stopping smoking is one of the main worries while quitting. Though most people do, you don't need to be concerned about this. Women, in particular, experience fear while considering leaving. This extra weight is just transitory, though.

However, I would argue that giving up smoking does come with extra baggage. Your body is temporarily attempting to adjust to life without cigarettes and the substances they are associated with. But the excess weight you gain will go away as time passes and your body adjusts to the new arrangement. It is ridiculous to use this as justification to keep smoking; being overweight is far less dangerous for your health and well-being than the harmful substances cigarettes contain. Similarly, it would help if you didn't ever worry about gaining weight.

You're gaining the extra weight primarily because your body is progressively searching for a replacement for your lack of smoking. After that, consider engaging in some simple activity while completing this procedure. Fortunately, being a tiny guy meant that stopping smoking wouldn't allow me to gain the extra weight; instead, I had to eat a lot more.

Get rid of all of your cigarettes. Store your ashtrays away.

Adapt your morning schedule. If you eat breakfast in the kitchen, move around the table. Stay occupied.

When the impulse to smoke strikes, find a substitute activity.

Keep other items in your mouth at all times, such as a toothpick, gum, or hard candies.

Reward yourself for not smoking. Watch a movie or take your pet out to eat.

Staying silent

If you find yourself feeling drowsier or angrier than usual, don't worry; these emotions will pass.

Make an effort to exercise; go on bike rides or walks.

If you're feeling tense, try to stay occupied, think of solutions to the problem, convince yourself that smoking won't help, and do something else.

Eat at regular intervals. Sometimes, the desire to smoke is confused with hunger.

With the money you save by not buying cigarettes, start a money jar.

Inform others that you've given up smoking, and the majority of people will be supportive. Your smoking pals may be curious about your quitting strategy. Speaking with others about your quitting is a terrific idea.

It's okay if you make a mistake and start smoking. Many ex-smokers made multiple attempts at quitting before they were successful. Give up once more.

Final Thoughts

You may notice an immediate improvement in your ability to taste and smell food after quitting smoking. It smells better on your breath. Your cough goes away. All ages of men and women experience this, including older people. Both healthy people and those who already have a sickness or condition brought on by smoking experience it.

Current smokers are less healthy than former smokers. Compared to current smokers, ex-smokers experience fewer sick days, health problems, and cases of pneumonia and bronchitis.

It costs less money to stop smoking.

See your doctor if you require additional assistance.

To help you overcome your addiction to smoking, they can recommend nicotine gum or a nicotine patch.

Methods And Structures For Quitting Smoking

When trying to quit smoking, the cravings to smoke can get to you. The majority of smokers experience significant passions or inclinations to smoke. Regardless, you are not powerless in the face of these desires.

When the urge to smoke arises, keep in mind that, whether you smoke or not, it will probably pass in five to ten minutes, even if it may very well be severe. You are getting closer to quitting smoking permanently each time you resist the urge to smoke.

Here are some strategies to help you resist the needing strikes temptation to smoke.

Treatment for nicotine replacement

Learn more about the treatment known as nicotine replacement. The options include:
• Nicotine spray or inhaler; • Nicotine gum, patches, and capsules available over-the-counter.
• Non-nicotine smoking cessation method.

Most of the time, these short-acting medications are safe to combine with long-acting nicotine patches or prescriptions that don't include nicotine. Nowadays, there has been a lot of thought given to using electronic cigarettes as an alternative to traditional cigarettes.

2. Steer clear of triggers

Your inclinations towards tobacco use are most likely to be rooted in the situations in which you have smoked or nibbled tobacco most frequently, such as social events or bars, when you're nervous or enjoying an espresso. Recognise your trigger situations and have a plan in place to avoid them either entirely or get through them without using tobacco.

Aim to avoid creating the conditions for a smoking relapse. For example,

If you think you will give in to your craving for tobacco, tell yourself that you should first stand by for ten more minutes - and then find something to do with your time during that period. Try visiting a public area that is smoke-free. These simple antics could even ruin your craving for tobacco.

4. Graze it

Give your lips something to do when you crave tobacco. Suck on hard candies or sugar-free gum, or munch on raw carrots, celery, almonds, or sunflower seeds for a satisfying crunch.

5. Aim to avoid having "only one."

One cigarette could tempt you to indulge in a tobacco yearning. Either way, don't fool yourself into thinking that you can end it there. Generally speaking, having just one leads to many, and you may find yourself smoking again.

6. Take action

Getting a job can help you deflect and weaken your tobacco-related desires. In fact, even a brief burst of vigorous activity, such as repeatedly sprinting up and down the stairs, can cause a tobacco craving to go. Go for a run or a walk outside.

If you are confined to your house or place of employment, try squats, deep knee bends, pushups, running squats, or walking up and down a series of steps. If you are not interested in doing active work, try praying, needlework, woodworking, or journaling. Alternatively, complete interruption-prone jobs like vacuuming or filing desk work.

7. Use relaxing techniques

You may have relied on smoking as a coping mechanism for stress. It could be upsetting in and of itself to oppose a tobacco desire. Provide some respite from tension by using relaxation techniques such as deep breathing exercises, yoga, massages

8. Make a fortification request

Get assistance from a family member, friend, or member of a support group in your efforts to resist a tobacco need. Call someone, go for a walk, exchange a few giggles, or get together to commiserate about your desires.

9. Seek assistance online

Participate in an online programme to help people quit smoking. Alternatively, visit the blog of a slacker and provide motivating comments for someone else who might be struggling with tobacco cravings. Learn from how others have satisfied their lusts for tobacco.

10. Assist yourself in recalling the benefits

Jot down or openly express the reasons you must give up smoking in order to resist your cravings for tobacco. These could be:
• Having a positive feeling • Recovering quickly • Protecting your loved ones from secondhand smoke • Saving money

Remember that attempting to overcome a desire is always preferable than doing nothing at all. Additionally, every time you resist a craving for smoke, you get closer to quitting altogether.

11. Honour your victories

remained cigarette-free for the entire day? Treat yourself to something extraordinary. Withstood the week? Add up all the money you have saved by refusing to accept smokes. Put the money away for future use or use the reserve for a particular pleasure.

Reward yourself for quitting smoking by completing an activity you enjoy every day, such as spending more time with your children or grandchildren, attending a ball game, taking a walk, relaxing in the tub, or watching a movie. Your goal to permanently quit smoking can be achieved with the help of all your small wins.

Propranol

a medication that acts as an aminoketone antidepressant. It affects the noradrenergic and dopaminergic nervous systems. Dopamine and norepinephrine are crucial for the emergence of nicotine dependence. Nicotine causes the release of these and other neurotransmitters.

Norepinephrine released in the locus coeruleus triggers higher cortical activities such as focus, memory, and attention. Moreover, nicotine increases the pleasure of using the drug by stimulating the production of dopamine in the nucleus acumens, the brain's reward centre. Though not significantly, bupropion blocks dopamine and norepinephrine from being reabsorbed at synapses.

Furthermore, it has been shown that the drug inhibits the activity of the nicotinic acetylcholine receptor. The medication may lessen withdrawal symptoms, according to its several modes of action. Increased dopamine levels in the brain may continue to activate pleasure-response areas even in the absence of nicotine.

Studies indicate bupropion may have fewer adverse effects than other smoking cessation drugs, including weight gain. It is advised to begin treatment with 150 mg once day in the morning for the first three to four days. An additional 150 mg is taken in the evening if this is effective. During the first week of treatment, patients are allowed to smoke until a steady level of bupropion is achieved.

Patients should decide to stop smoking during the second week. Treatment can last three to four months (six to twelve months for certain people). Bupropion plus nicotine replacement therapy may be required for smokers who have relapsed or who were unable to quit with just nicotine replacement therapy.

This drug is usually well tolerated and has a low incidence of side effects. The most frequently reported side effects are dry mouth (10%), headache (10%), and insomnia (35–40%). Bupropion lowers the threshold for seizures, so patients who are at risk for seizures shouldn't use it.

About 0.1% of those using bupropion will have a seizure. This drug receives excellent scores for its effects on the heart. There is no evidence to suggest that taking this drug raises the risk of dying suddenly. Individuals who have previously received treatment with bupropion do not have a decreased likelihood of effectively stopping this medication.

After a year of usage, the abstinence rates for nicotine patches were 10.1%, nicotine gum was 10.8%, nicotine inhalation was 10.5% to 10.9%, and bupropion was 18.5% to 23.0%.

Diverticline

Both the want to smoke and the withdrawal symptoms are lessened. Treatment will start the week before the intended date of cessation. Take 0.5 mg twice day orally for the first three days; 0.5 mg twice day for days four through seven; and 1 mg twice day for the remaining twelve weeks. Twelve weeks further of therapy could be given to reduce the chance of a recurrence further.

Your most excellent option if you want to stop smoking and stay away from bupropion is varenicline. Adverse drug effects are frequently favourable. The most frequent negative impact is nausea, however taking the medication with food and liquids dramatically reduces this risk.

Alternative Forms of Medicine

Two short trials that started 10–28 days before the stopping date and used 75–100 mg of nortriptyline daily for three months showed that the medication was helpful in helping people stop smoking. It has not been demonstrated that using any other antidepressant or anxiolytic medication helps people quit smoking.

Even though clonidine treatment with 0.1-0.4 mg/day for 2-6 weeks lessens nicotine withdrawal symptoms and has been shown helpful for smoking cessation, the medication's high frequency of side effects, such as dry mouth, drowsiness, and constipation, limited its utilisation.

A serotonergic agonist and anxiolytic; this best characterises buspirone. Some people have taken 15–30 mg daily, divided up, to help with smoking withdrawal. It won't make you fall asleep or connect you to anything. It hasn't been demonstrated to be helpful in aiding smokers in quitting, though.

Naltrexone is the long-acting form of the opioid agonist naloxone. Research indicates that it can assist female smokers who are depressed in quitting. The adverse effects of the medication include nausea, vomiting, drowsiness, and stomach pain. This medicine has to be studied in a sizable randomised controlled trial before it can be regularly recommended to help individuals stop smoking.

Mecamylamine functions as a non-competitive blocker of nicotine receptors, hence it doesn't induce withdrawal symptoms. Silver acetate can be taken orally by tablets or gum. It creates an unpleasant taste when combined with the sulphides in cigarette smoke, but sadly, the medication has a relatively low compliance rate. Although attempts have been made, using synthetic tobacco substitutes like cellulose has proven to be unsuccessful.

vaccine against nicotine

Nicotine antibodies counteract the drug's addictive properties by preventing its transportation to the brain. Three nicotine vaccines are in investigation at the moment. These immunisations hold potential for treating and preventing relapses following smoking cessation.

Treatment with Multiple Drugs

Combination nicotine replacement therapy (NRT) may be helpful for smokers with moderate to high nicotine dependency who have attempted and failed to stop with monotherapy, mainly if they had severe withdrawal symptoms.

Clinical Counseling/Medication

Any doctor should begin with the five A's: ask, counsel, assess, assist, and arrange.

Recommendation: Physicians ought to firmly advise patients to give up smoking after ascertaining their current tobacco use status. Even with a brief medical advice to stop, higher rates of smoking cessation are demonstrated.

Assess: The patient's financial status, the health of the patient's family members, and the patient's current state of illness should all be connected to the patient's tobacco use.

Help: The patient and the therapist should collaborate to develop a quitting plan. The patient ought to set a date for quitting and intend to stop in one to two weeks. The patient needs to let their loved ones and coworkers know that they are trying to quit smoking and to ask for their support.

A patient should be ready for any challenges that may arise during the first few weeks of their attempt to quit smoking, such as withdrawal symptoms like depression, cravings to smoke, and difficulties focusing. The patient should cut off all access to tobacco products and avoid smoking in places with lots of traffic before attempting to quit (e.g., work, home, and car).

Those who smoke more than ten cigarettes a day and those who are pregnant or nursing should receive pharmacotherapy in order to quit; otherwise, light smokers and minors should not receive this treatment. bupropion SR, nicotine gum, nicotine inhaler, nicotine nasal spray, and nicotine patch. Factors like cost, physician familiarity with the medications, contraindications for specific patients, patient preference, and previous patient experience with a particular pharmacotherapy (positive or negative) should inform the selection of a particular therapy. (eg, history of depression, concerns about weight gain).

Establish A Clear Goal About Smoking

We discuss objectives and routines a lot, but it's crucial that we both understand each other when I use terms, so that when I do, you know what I mean.

For example, a goal is the overall result you wish to accomplish in life. It's the way you relate to your mission. That's the change you want to go through. In this instance, quitting smoking is your main objective.

And the key to this procedure is a habit. It is the daily work towards achieving that objective.

Goals are much more exciting than habits, but in the end, your daily actions define your potential for success in life. Now that we know your ultimate objective, we need to dissect it into manageable daily routines.

You discovered throughout your one-day quit that smoking is a collection of tiny habits. It's a sequence of times during the day when you choose whether or not to smoke. Despite having a severe pattern of smoking two or three packs a day, you are not genuinely smoking for the majority of the day.

You are able to abstain from smoking for significant portions of your day. If your habit persists and you're further along the path, the first thing we need to do is break and change your morning routine. You'll find that if you break the first behaviour in a chain, the rest of the procedure becomes shockingly simple. We may layer positive habits throughout the day to reinforce and build upon that one powerful habit.

Establishing Daily Health Routines

Fundamentally, habits are just the daily performance of a personally significant goal—note the term "personally" here. It indicates that you connect with the objective. We must thus choose the appropriate one. You know what your personal goal is now that you've finished the procedure and have a vision board up on your wall. We take each day as it comes, and you are aware that immediate gratification frequently outweighs long-term gain.

The power of little acts is in connecting the underlying reasons for your desire to better the area of your life. Consider what your life might be like if you started every day with tiny deeds that would eventually lead to a cascade of advantageous outcomes. You create your workday by concentrating on the most crucial duties after eating a nutritious breakfast and enjoying an excellent talk with your loved ones. Then, you carry out additional routines that support your primary objectives throughout the day. I assure you that you would have greater fulfilment, achieve more, and have a more positive direction for your career. You can do all of this if you concentrate on little tasks that are connected to your significant objectives.

There needs to be more work involved in these habits. Actually, the majority can be finished in five minutes or less. Nevertheless, if you repeat them frequently enough, they have a potent compounding effect.

Apply the Framework for S.M.A.R.T. Goals.

This term could be familiar to you from somewhere else. S.M.A.R.T. is a highly focused approach to goal setting. George T. Doran originally penned it in a November 1981 issue of Management Review. Allow me to walk you through S.M.A.R.T. S - Specific in five letters. You want something precise that makes sense, is easy to understand, meaningful, and makes it clear what your objective is. It's acceptable if our aim is to "stop smoking," but we need be a little more specific. One standard error people make when trying to reduce weight is not writing down a target weight. We're hedging our bets if we don't make it clear, and we might give up after only a minor victory.

That is the issue of having a vague objective. Since we're breaking a habit in this instance, we may be really explicit and even break it by stating, "I want to go from three packs a day to one pack a day." We can declare, "I want to cut down from a pack a day to five cigarettes a day," after achieving that initial objective.

Measurable, or M. A goal needs to be quantifiable, which implies it needs to have a numerical value. Saying I want to lose ten pounds and losing three means I'm thirty percent of the way there. For this reason, even if your ultimate objective is to give up smoking entirely, I want you to keep track of how many cigarettes you smoke each day and use that as a starting point. Your aim is now quantifiable.

Most of the time, we declare our intention to stop smoking, but after only one cigarette, we feel like complete failures. This is due to the fact that our objectives are brittle and our will to give up can break at any time. If your aim is measurable, you have a higher chance of success.

A: Achievable / Attainable. You can actually accomplish this aim throughout this cycle. It's too much to go from smoking three or five packs a day to none in one day if you do that. Our goal is to develop a schedule that works well for you. You should slightly reposition your goals during this process. It may take five months, even though you initially said it would take three. That's adaptation, not giving up. However, it's also possible that you're ahead of schedule.

R: Reasonable or Relevant. A goal that aligns with our purpose is what we seek. Naturally, you've already arrived, as this book focuses on a specific kind of objective, and each of the reasons we've discussed is closely related to it. You're already in a relevant place.

T: Sensitive to Time. For me, this is the most crucial section. All you need to be S.M.A.R.T. is a goal that is time-sensitive, quantifiable, and specified. I'll explain why. I may tell you, "My goal is to lose thirty pounds in thirty days," instead of, "My goal is to lose weight." You are able to assess my success not just after thirty days but also by looking at the amount of weight I have dropped. I would have lost six-sevenths of the way there if I had shed twenty-six pounds. That is quite good!

Please permit me to discuss some specific S.M.A.R.T. objectives related to smoking with you. Here is the last set of examples to help you focus on your first smart objective, in case I still need to give you more by now.

Give off smoking in ninety days or less.

Within thirty days, transition to 50% vaping.

Within sixty days, make the switch to vaping exclusively.

Transform before Christmas from reds to lights.

I spent $100 less on cigarettes each month.

In order to have quantifiable objectives, we are going to use some of those other approaches at this point. The nice thing is that you can goal-stack in the same way that you habit-stack. After completing and accomplishing a goal, you're prepared to move on to the next. It's possible that using some of those other strategies—like vaping or group support—will be necessary for you to bridge yourself.

Using one of these tools to help you stop smoking will be your first objective; after that, you'll want to eliminate the need for the tool. You can eventually stop vaping and stop smoking altogether even if you start by replacing smoking with vaping.

Shall we take complete charge now?

Smoking and well-being

Cigars, pipe tobacco, and chewing tobacco were the most popular tobacco products during the beginning of the 20th century. While smoking was starting to rise sharply, the mass production of cigarettes was still in its infancy. As stated in the Encyclopaedia Britannica's ninth edition (1888), tobacco was thought to have some medical qualities in addition to being suspected of having some negative health consequences. At the time, a lot of academics and medical professionals supported tobacco usage since it had benefits including improved mood, less boredom, and increased performance.

Contrarily, by the early 21st century, tobacco smoking was known to be highly addictive and one of the leading causes of illness and death worldwide. Furthermore, the number of smoking-related deaths annually was predicted to rise sharply in the 21st century due to the late 20th-century rapid increase in smoking in developing nations. For instance, the World Health Organisation (WHO) calculated that four million deaths worldwide were attributed to tobacco usage annually in the late 1990s. In 2003 and 2011, this forecast was raised to roughly five million, and by 2030, it was predicted to reach six million annually. It was expected that 80 percent of those fatalities will take place in emerging nations. In fact, tobacco usage was still rising in South America, Asia, and Africa even as it was declining in many western European, North American, and Australian countries.

produced using a variety of additives to extend the shelf life of the tobacco, change how it burns, regulate the moisture content, prevent insect eggs from hatching that might be present in the plant material, cover up the irritating effects of nicotine, and add any number of flavours and fragrances. When tobacco and these additives burn, more than 4,000 different chemical components are released into the smoke. Numerous of these substances are extremely harmful and have a variety of adverse health impacts.

Nicotine, tar (a combustion-related particulate residue), and gases including carbon dioxide and carbon monoxide are the main ingredients of tobacco smoke. In comparison to many other poisons found in tobacco smoke, nicotine's hazardous effect as a component of the smoke is typically regarded as minimal, even though it can be dangerous at very high quantities. Nicotine's primary negative impact on health is its addictive nature. The effects of carbon monoxide on health are severe and immediate. It readily exits the lungs and enters the bloodstream, On the haemoglobin molecule, carbon monoxide replaces oxygen and is only gradually eliminated. As a result, smokers commonly have elevated carbon monoxide levels, which deprive the body of oxygen and severely tax the cardiovascular system. Smoking has negative impacts that extend beyond the smoker. In addition to the smoke that a smoker inhales, other forms of tobacco smoke are similarly harmful: secondhand smoke

Cigarette smoking is prohibited by clean air legislation, which are becoming more common. These regulations, which were primarily enacted in the 1980s and 1990s, mandated the establishment of nonsmoking spaces in restaurants and workplaces. However, even stricter prohibitions were passed as it was discovered that the carcinogens in ambient smoke could readily spread throughout broad areas. Complete smoking bans in eateries, bars, and enclosed workplaces have been enacted since 2000 in a large number of cities, states, and regions throughout the world, including New York City in 2003, Scotland in 2006, Nairobi in 2007, and Chicago in 2008. One-third of the world's smokers reside in China, where a 2011 ban on smoking in public places, including restaurants and hotels, was enacted; the rule did not address smoking in workplaces or outline punishments.

Furthermore, entire nations—Ireland, Norway, and New Zealand in 2004; France and India in 2008—have banned smoking in restaurants, workplaces, and, in certain situations, in all public locations. Bhutan became the first nation to outlaw the selling of tobacco products and the smoking of tobacco products in public areas in 2005.

Adverse effects of smoking on health
Addiction, or more accurately, dependence, is a significant health consequence associated with tobacco use in all its forms. While addiction by itself is not fatal, it does play a role in tobacco-related deaths and illnesses by

encouraging smokers to stick with their habit, which exposes them to the chemicals in tobacco smoke on a regular basis. The Office of the Surgeon General in the United States, the Royal Society of Canada, from which blood quickly carries it to the brain, until the 1980s, despite numerous historical accounts of tobacco use's apparent ability to escalate into addiction for some smokers.

All of the physiological and behavioural symptoms that are typical of addiction are brought on by nicotine. These consequences include the stimulation of reward circuits in the brain, which results in physiological cravings and behavioural effects that lead to chronic use, tolerance, and physical dependence, as well as withdrawal symptoms upon cessation. The numerous components of tobacco smoke that, for many, offer enjoyable sensory qualities and intensify the effects of nicotine also play a role in tobacco addiction. Ammonia, menthol, levulinic acid, and even chocolate are among the ingredients that enhance the flavour and aroma of cigarettes. Compared to nicotine treatments like gum and patches, which have less appealing and lower sensory effects, cigarettes are more addictive. (See the section about quitting smoking below.)

When smoke that has high levels of nicotine is breathed deeply, the lungs absorb the drug quickly; the nicotine diffuses into the bloodstream just as soon as oxygen does. In less than ten seconds, nicotine travels from the lungs to the brain. Nicotine binds to receptor proteins on the surface A nicotine molecule attaches itself to a nicotine receptor on a neuron, causing the neuron to send a nerve impulse to a target organ or tissue. Nicotine's physiological and psychological impacts result from the release of neurotransmitters, which are chemical messengers stimulated by this process. For instance, nicotine stimulates the adrenal glands, causing the release of norepinephrine and adrenaline, which elevate blood pressure and heart rate while enhancing alertness and focus. In the brain, nicotine also promotes the release of the neurotransmitter dopamine.

Remind yourself of its advantages.
Put your reasons for wanting to quit smoking in writing or state them aloud. These causes could consist of:

Having improved
Gaining well-being
Keeping your family members away from secondhand smoke
How tobacco products are created

We consider the components of cigarettes to be so familiar. The smoker frequently overlooks the fact that it is actually a sophisticated industrial product with countless varieties. There are three components to every cigarette. Tobacco is the most crucial factor. The majority of cigarettes on the market are made from a blend of dried tobaccos that vary in terms of the plant variety as well as the method of manufacture: some are dried in dryers with controlled humidity and temperature, others are dried in the sun, and still others are smoked. Expanded and reconstituted tobacco can also be found in cigarettes; this is "reconstituted" tobacco processing waste that is sealed in foil using a variety of physical and chemical techniques that include the use of materials like freon and carbon dioxide. Paper is the second component of a cigarette; it serves as more than just a covering; it also controls combustion and alters the smoking experience. Its porosity is a critical factor because the more air that can move through the paper, the more the smoke chemicals that are diluted as they pass through the cigarette. The filter comes last and is most frequently composed of cellulose acetate fibres bonded together with triacetin, a hardening agent that helps the filter keep its shape. However, what additives are in cigarettes? Cigarettes, like food, are the product of an industrial process that uses materials other than raw materials but is necessary to maximise production efficiency, increase product yield, and satisfy consumer preferences. The chemicals employed for these reasons are called additives. In order to streamline the manufacturing of cigarettes, additives are used, such as to lessen the brittleness of seasoned tobacco. Several compounds that contain ethyl alcohol, carbon dioxide, and ammonia are included in this group. Ammonium and sodium phosphate, sodium citrate, and potassium citrate are a few of the additives that are used to help with combustion. Alternatively, the flavour of cigarettes is enhanced by other additives, which cover up the wrong notes and add new ones. They include things like cocoa, licorice, honey, fruit extracts, and different spices. Then, the additives are also used to: maintain the tobacco's moisture content and flexibility; prevent the growth of mould by using preservatives; boost the tobacco's mass by using chemically inert materials; and maximise the release of nicotine by using compounds that contain ammonia.

Thus, acknowledging your responsibility to yourself comes first in the second step to quitting smoking. You wish to live a long and happy life. Because if you really did, you would have overdosed on something cheap, jumped in front of a speeding train, or taken a gun to your head. But here you are, alive. Really, you don't want to die. You wish to pass away at a healthy age. Thus, smoking is similar to accelerating the process. It resembles a samurai using a blunt knife to commit kamikaze. Smoking causes issues that will undoubtedly bring you there in shatters and groans. It takes care of your descent into the afterlife. You become irresponsible to yourself when you smoke. You become reliant on smoking to provide you with a false sense of security, comfort, clothing, and confidence, making you feel like a baby. You smoke for a variety of reasons, including self-defense, social disobedience, breaking moral and conventional rules, and situational identification. You have given up smoking. You sure can. Yea-ou... Ca-an

What Makes You Want To Give Up Smoking?

Making the decision to stop and understanding your motivations are the first steps towards quitting. What makes you want to give up smoking? Is your goal to become healthier the reason? Is it your intention to cut costs? Is it your desire to build stronger bonds with friends and family on a personal level?

Whatever your motivation, you must use it to spur you to break this risky habit. To get clarity, you can ask yourself multiple questions if you are unsure of your motivations.

To begin with, what do you find objectionable about smoking, and what do you lose out on each time you light up? How does smoking impact your finances, career, and health, among other aspects of your life? If you keep smoking, what do you think will happen to you and your family? When you give up smoking, how do you think your life will improve?

You need to constantly remind yourself of your reason once you've discovered what it is. You must write it down and place it in a visible location.

If there are multiple reasons, make a list and stick it to your refrigerator door, desktop, or dresser mirror so you can easily remember it. It can also be kept in your car or any other location where you typically store your cigarettes.

Giving up smoking can improve your appearance and well-being.

You'll have a lower chance of developing cancer, heart disease, and other ailments. In addition to having a lower chance of getting the flu or a cold, you will be able to bounce back from illnesses more quickly. Breathing will become easier for you. You'll have a decrease in blood pressure. Your teeth and fingernails won't be stained anymore. Also, your skin will appear healthier.

Giving up smoking can enhance your way of life.

More money will be available for savings or more significant purchases. You'll have more time to spend with the people you care about. Both your productivity at work and the amount of time you have for your hobbies will increase. Additionally, you'll be able to smell everything and smell better overall. You won't feel self-conscious about your offensive odor. Furthermore, you won't need to consider when or where you can smoke.

Your family life can be better if you give up smoking.

Your ability to lead by example will improve for your kids. They'll be grateful that you're trying to give up. Your accomplishments will make your friends, family, and even coworkers proud.

Your family will also be healthier because you won't be exposing them to secondhand smoke. Furthermore, you won't persuade anyone to take up your bad habit. Along with having more energy to finish your tasks, you'll also have more time to engage in your favorite activities.

Giving up smoking will eliminate the danger of secondhand smoke to others.

Contrary to popular belief, secondhand smoke poses a greater risk than you may imagine. You see, other people also suffer from the harmful effects of smoking. Every time you light up, you also endanger the safety of those in your immediate vicinity.

The harmful substances found in secondhand smoke also referred to as environmental tobacco smoke, include benzene, ammonia, cyanide, formaldehyde, polonium, chromium, and cyanide. These are the same compounds that are present in petrol, cleaning supplies, and chemical weapons, among other things.

Cancer, heart disease, lung disease, infections, and other chronic diseases are brought on by secondhand smoke toxins. It poses a particular risk to expectant mothers and children.

The Ex-Smoker

Today, the majority of smoking cessation programs are designed to assist smokers in quitting. From the moment they wake up until they go to bed, ex-smokers only THINK about smoking. They fail because of this.

The majority of smoking cessation programs have a success rate of less than 10%, and the smoker's payment amount has no bearing on the program's success rate.

You may have participated in a program that makes you consider smoking. Here are a few indicators that a program may be designed for former smokers.

First of all, each time you purchase cigarettes, you are instructed to change brands. If you have been smoking regular-flavour cigarettes, you are then required to switch to mentholated cigarettes. If you typically smoke filtered cigarettes, you are then required to smoke unfiltered ones. It is recommended that you smoke with the opposite hand from your typical smoking hand.

If you usually hold the cigarette between your index and middle fingers, you are instructed to keep it between your little finger and your thumb. Then, instead of placing the cigarette in the middle of your lips, you are told to put it on the left or right side. It is required that you maintain a journal in which you should record your feelings and thoughts as well as the date, time, and location of each cigarette session.

So, what are your plans for the rest of the day? You'll be considering taking a cigarette. That is too much for humans to handle. Ex-smokers return to smoking because they are compelled to do so. Willpower alone is insufficient to overcome the obsession.

Because they make smokers think about smoking all the time, nicotine gum, patches, and inhalers also have meager success rates. A smoker feels about smoking every time they apply the patch or chew a piece of nicotine gum.

A woman once called me to ask for a meeting regarding her "chocolate problem." According to her admission, she was "addicted to chocolate" to the point where she would think about chocolate all day long, starting at night. She had to have chocolate because her craving for it was so intense.

In every other regard, she was sophisticated, intelligent, well-educated, and in complete control of herself. She was keeping an eye on her weight and was aware that overeating chocolate would undermine her physical fitness regimen. She would always come home from grocery shopping with at least one enormous chocolate bar in her bag. She would convince herself that the chocolate couldn't defeat her.

After putting the chocolate bar in her kitchen cabinet, she would try to carry on with her day. She soon found, though, that her only focus was on that candy bar.

While attempting to watch TV, her thoughts would constantly return to the chocolate. When she was upset, she would tell herself that she was in charge. She would get up, grab the chocolate bar, remove the wrapper, inspect it, inhale the scent, and then return it to the cabinet.

She would try to do something again, but her thoughts would always return to that chocolate bar. She told me that after she went to bed with her husband, she would think about the chocolate bar while he attempted to make love to her.

She would get out of bed, go back into the kitchen, grab the candy bar, and toss it into the trash can because this made her even more angry with herself. She would tell herself, as she went back to bed, that she was in charge of herself.

She would get out of bed, return to the kitchen, and gaze at the chocolate bar in the trash a few minutes later. Giving in to the temptation, she would take the bar from the garbage and promise herself she would only eat one bite. She would eat one bite and then feel so guilty that she would toss the rest in the trash and go back to bed.

She would go to the kitchen once more, get the chocolate bar, and eat it like an animal with no pleasure or enjoyment after thinking about the chocolate for a few minutes until she could take it no more.

Is this something you recognize? Have you ever thrown away your cigarettes and promised yourself that you would try to stop smoking, only to find that you couldn't stop thinking about them all the time? Then you bought, borrowed, or stole a cigarette, smoked it right away, and became hooked again.

You smoked more after that than you had previously.

Ex-smokers are drawn to smoking, much like a moth to a flame. It is not just you. You make sense to me. This program is unique in that it helps you get rid of the desire to smoke by making you forget about your cigarettes and never want to repurchase one.

This book teaches you how to quit smoking, not how to become an ex-smoker. The best part is that you won't experience anxiety, irritability, or smoking obsession.

You're not going to consider smoking. You won't feel resentful, cheated, or depressed, and you won't put on weight unless you choose to. You will no longer have the smoking habit in your life or the past. You won't ever again feel the need to smoke. Furthermore, you won't turn into a changed smoker.

The Advantages Of Maintaining Your Quit Smoking Habit

Give up smoking and make a positive change.

For some people, quitting smoking might be about staying healthy. Still, in reality, there are many advantages that you can anticipate, experience, and delight in once you're fully committed to sticking with it.

Savour an Expanded Life

To see your grandchildren grow up and mature, you must start smoking as early as possible. Smoking can increase the risk of dying as much as ten times earlier due to the different life experiences caused by smoking-related injuries that are linked to unhealthy habits.

Reduce Your Risk of Experiencing Various Health Conditions Smoking cigarettes can put your life and your quality of life at risk. There is a significant likelihood that you will have to deal with illness every single day. If you want your life to be healthy and free from various ailments like feminity issues, impotence, macular degeneration, cataracts, osteoporosis, tooth loss, and gum disease, make sure you give up smoking as soon as possible. Make your body as pure as a baby's.

Everyone loves babies, and by giving up smoking, you also increase the likelihood that your body will resemble that of a baby once more. Give up your smoking habit right away if you want to feel good and be pure like a baby. When you do this, it will only take a few minutes for you to return to your normal state, which includes your blood pressure, pulse rate, and regular hand and foot temperatures.

Give Your Honeymoon a Night to Remember Single Night: By quitting smoking, you also contribute to a better quality of life for yourself. For both sexes, abstaining from cigarettes can have significant advantages. Women will be harassed more frequently, and men will have better opportunities for employment. Furthermore, smoking won't make you appear more attractive in the eyes of the opposite sex.

Stop the Harsh Coughing

Due to your lungs' increased ability to function normally, both heavy breathing and breath shortage will subside simultaneously. When your lungs return to normal, it can improve lung function, clear the lungs, and reduce the likelihood of different types of infections.

Say Goodbye to Smoker's Stink: When you stop smoking, the smell will likely disappear from your body as well after a few minutes. Additionally, when you smell good, you'll also become more attractive to those around you because nobody would want to play around with someone whose scent is identical to that of a cinnamon stick. Not only that but when you smoke, your house will smell fresher and cleaner.

Look good and feel good.

No one enjoys premature aging, which is something that smoking can cause. It goes without saying that you would not want to be made to marry someone twice your age if you were still in your early 20s. When you quit smoking, it will not only benefit your general health but also enhance your overall appearance and appearance. Smoking can make you feel sluggish and uninteresting. Keep up your stopping resolution to feel and look better and see significant changes in your life.

www.ingramcontent.com/pod-product-compliance
Lightning Source LLC
Chambersburg PA
CBHW052201110526
44591CB00012B/2036